The Waning Wisp

The Waning Wisps of Withered Wishes

A Record of an Absence

Deepak M. Babu

Copyright © 2019 by Deepak M. Babu

All rights reserved. This book or any portion thereof may not be reproduced or used in any manner whatsoever without the express written permission of the author except for the use of brief quotations in a book review.

First Printing, 2019

ISBN: 9781099884207

Email me at: deepakmbabu@gmail.com

Visit my blog at: **purposescrossed.wordpress.com**

Cover art by Mercy Kurian (mercysown@yahoo.com)

For
Alyssa, Anezka, Prayerna, and Anastasia
(Dad's four angels)

May you find comfort
Through every day and even
Joy and health and peace

Preface

When this collection of poems is published, it will have been three years since Dad passed away. At the risk of sounding clichéd, it seems like yesterday that I was with him in the hospital talking about what life would be like when he returned home. In a matter of days, those wishes had withered away, the wisps of their memories waning with each passing day.

I began to write these poems on the day after Dad passed away and I shared some of them with my family and some friends. A few of them suggested that I get the poems published. At first, I recoiled at the idea. These poems were too close to my heart. Their words were infused with the anguish I felt at Dad's passing and I did not know if I wanted to allow strangers into the private reaches of my grief.

I don't know what made me change my mind but as the third anniversary of Dad's passing approached I found myself thinking about publishing the collection. The poems helped me work through and deal with my grief and I think they may have some benefit for others.

So here are the poems I wrote in the wake of Dad's demise. They constitute, as the subtitle of the collection suggests, a record of an absence.

The world seems smaller
(27 June 2016)

The world seems smaller
No more it holds the joy and
Warmth within his smile

Forever Thankful
(27 June 2016)

'Tis a day that's like no other
The first time in my life
I wake up just as usual
But grief and sorrow rife

A morn with no precedence
Though the sun rises once more
The dawn now gone behind us
Having shocked me to my core

The world seems somewhat lighter
Yet heavier the same
Light because there's lesser
Heavy, my grief to blame

The world seems ever poorer
Richer the heavens still
For someone went between them
Mine, a hole that can't be filled

Oh dad, my father, dearest
What pain you leave behind
But I forever thankful
A dad like you was mine

On Singing for Dad's Homecoming
(6 July 2016)

Did you hear me as I sang
Though soft my voice was then
Or did you only hear the heav'nly
Voices that beckoned

Did the words I voiced somehow
Reach deep into your soul
Did I sing in futility
Did the song achieve its goal

Though what I sang was hymns
That spoke God's glory true
What I was singing though unsaid
Was just my, "I love you."

So did that thought reach into you
And did it touch your heart
Did my song of farewell
Speak to you when you did depart

Incorruptible
(6 July 2016)

Incorruptible in life were you
Incorruptible now in death
Unshakeable from your convictions
Up until your final breath

Yet though so strong, gentle you were
With those with love you blest
What memories you leave with us
This flood can't be repressed

And neither would we want to stanch
This flow on salty cheeks
For deep within our hearts we find
Its source if we but seek

Your fight now done, you've gone ahead
Our waiting now does start
To see your face, to feel your arms
To hear your beating heart

You won't return who loved us deep
Loved each moment dear
But since we'll soon see you again
This hope dispels all fear

Goodbyes Unsaid
(7 July 2016)

Wrecked by this thought that we said not goodbye
To you as you went from us into your rest
That we should have had the chance to be nigh
Bid farewell to you. We thought that was best.
We wanted occasion to tie up loose ends
Like in the fictions we watch on the screen.
We each say some words, then to God commend
Your life, your spirit, tears no more unseen.
But now looking back that seems quite unreal.
Would we ever have sensed time opportune?
Your going, to the end, to us so surreal.
No matter how late would have been yet too soon.
And so we rest with this hope ringing true
Goodbyes were unsaid since we will see you.

The Lament of 2202[1]
(14 July 2016)

What shall my walls say
Of this month
Your voice we did not hear
The floors whisper 'bout
Not feeling
Your footsteps loud and clear
My windows look out
To a world
That's now to you gone blind
The door through which
You walked a month
Away for the last time
What can I say now
Of this month
Of not being home to you
The only solace
One comfort
You've gone to your home true

---

[1] Dad and Mom lived in an apartment numbered 2202.

Trapped Within Time
(15 July 2016)

You were nearby when my first breath I drew
And I was with you when you last breathed that day
Your arms embraced me to this world anew
But mine had to release and send you away
My entry did make you with smiles to beam
But I told them to move your lips so you 'smiled'
You carried me gently; you lay me to dream
I saw you belabored in bed for a while
You rocked me to sleep and you sang me your songs
I sang to you hoping for the absurd
For years you did listen, lent your ears so long
While now mine just wanted you to say a word
What contrasts between your experience and mine
You gone now from me while I'm trapped within time

How Heavy is a Hole?
(20 July 2016)

How heavy is a hole?
How filling emptiness?
How numbing is this pain?
How noisy quietness?
How cold this burning loss?
How sweet these bitter tears?
How present this absence?
How minutes seem like years?
How feel the lack of touch?
How sightless now these eyes?
How alone in company?
How comfortless these sighs?
How joy amidst sorrow?
How future looking past?
How solace in tumult?
Since to be raised at last.

You Slipped Away From Me
(22 July 2016)

The words slip out from me
As I slip my fingers
Through your hair.
"They are coming," I say,
"Coming to see you
And to say goodbye.
Will you not
Stay a little longer, please?

"What will I say to them
If you have already gone
When they finally arrive?
They are coming," I say,
"They will arrive,
Now rushing through
The unmoving traffic.
So stay a little longer, please."

But, I think, you hear
The cries of jubilation,
The heralds' proclamation
Announcing your arrival,
"He is coming," they say.
And as, through your hair,
I slipped my fingers
You slipped away from me.

Safe In The Arms Of Jesus
[An Acrostic]
(22 July 2016)

Suddenly you have been taken from me
And now the waiting begins
For how much longer I just cannot see
Each day the vacuum sets in
I do not know if I did what was right
Nor were there paths for to take
That would have seen you be still in my sight
Heavy this thought my heart breaks
Expended for now my energy seems
All drained I am with the pain
Reflect again if my mind were not keen
My wish to see you again
Some may say I did not think of all ways
Or that I gave up too soon
For in the end this is what I can say
Just that your life was a boon
Each moment passes in agony still
Someday I know you'll see us
Understanding that you are then until
Safe in the arms of Jesus

Just One Day With You
(25 July 2016)

Five hundred, yes, and sixty four
The months I had with you
Another one has gone by too
Not like the ones before

The first ones had gone by so fast
I scarcely knew their end
The one that finally broke the trend
The one that went by last

Taken for granted all those ones
It seemed as there was time
To speak of everything sublime
With the rising moons and suns

But this month that's just gone by
Crawled by at a snail's pace
Each minute's pain barely could face
Why doesn't time now fly?

How am I now to face the new
Months in future's shade
Willingly all of them I'd trade
For just one day with you

The Minutes Dragged By
(25 July 2016)

The minutes dragged by
As though time itself were
Unwilling to move on.
His body, once vibrant,
Now lay inert, lifeless
On the hospital bed.
I looked down at him.
What did I chance to see?

The face that brought me joy
And that I brought joy to
Now lay motionless
Not recognizing me.
I touched his face,
His lips, his cheeks.

But where once I would
Feel the warmth of love
Now I could only feel
Unresponsiveness.

But still my hand strayed
On his unsmiling face
Just to get a final touch
Before a touch would only
Reveal he had truly gone
Into this last, cold sleep.

I Was There
(25 July 2016)

I was there.
For some reason
Some inexplicable reason,
Only I was
Given the honor
Of being there.
I was not the only one
Who wanted
To be there.
My mother, my sister
Her husband and daughters,
My wife and daughters,
Would have all wanted
To be there.
Or to be precise,
Though none of us wanted
It to happen,
Were it to happen,
We would all have wanted
To be there.
But only I was
Given the honor.
What kind of honor is this?
It is not the kind
One can brag about
Or boast about!
It is not the kind
One thinks back on
With a smile.

But at the same time,
It outstrips all other honors.
It is not something
One desires or wants.
But if it comes to you,
You accept it with
The deepest gratitude.
For in some strange way,
This too is a grace
Shown to me, that
I was there.

Work out the Details
(27 July 2016)

It was too difficult to pray.
The absence of Dad
Was palpable in the house.
What could I pray for?

Should I pray for
God to take me too
So I could see him again?
Was my grief so great
That I could pray for this
And thereby sentence
Those left behind
To bear additional grief?

Should I pray for
The end of the world
So I could see him again?

Was my pain so special
That it alone should
Precipitate such action
On God's part
Despite the fact that
There were countless others
Who had also experienced
Similar pain before?

Should I pray for...
What?

Ideas floated in my head
In those interminable
Contemplative moments,
One more outlandish
Than the next,
Each new one indicating
The desperation of
My heart,
The fragile hope
That still formed
A thread to grasp.

But in the end
Even the ideas ran out.
And so I simply prayed that
We would see him again
Let God work out the details.

Behind this Veil
(27 July 2016)

Look at me now with your questioning stare,
Wondering wherefore my eyes remain dry,
Thinking that I should openly declare
My pain and sorrow with ne'er ending sigh.
Do you yet wonder how composed I stay
With sobbing and shedding of tears all around?
Your eyes accuse me and claim that I may
Not be aggrieved since I make not a sound.
You may accuse me, yes, that is your right.
And mine the right not to pander to you.
For what you want is a blubbering sight;
Entertainment to prove my grief is true.
But all my tears hid from you without fail
Who cannot see what lies behind this veil.

I Let Them Linger
(30 July 2016)

My fingers still tingle
At the memory grave
Of touching your face
Trying to be brave

Shallow your breathing
Despite being forced
Pressureless blood
Through your veins coursed

Hopelessly hoping
A miracle now
Would turn the tables
And heal you somehow

I wanted you sorely
To return to me
But that wouldn't happen
Was clear I could see

I knew you were going
You started to sink
Unable to pull you
Back from the brink

Coming to accept
That you'd run your race
That now you would go
'Twas my turn to brace

So across your face
I ran my fingers
Not wanting goodbye
I let them linger

Now You Were Not
(30 July 2016)

You were there.
As I faced this trying time
You stayed with me
As I kept that final watch.
Without you I could not
Have stayed the course
Silently you buoyed my hopes
Wordlessly you stilled my fears
Peacefully you comforted
Giving me your strength
Maybe my spirit couldn't soar
But at least it did not sink
And then the watch ended
My hopes rendered hopeless
A while you were there
But now you were not

This Death In Sleep
(30 July 2016)

It hit me harder today -
Your absence.
Shouldn't it get easier
Am I not on the road
And is this not the path
To healing?

But the waking moments,
Weighed down by
The load unburdened
By the skies,
Seemed to have come
To a standstill.

And there was I
In the cold vice-like grip
Of unrelenting time -
Unwilling to give me up
Unable to take me on.

So there I was
Living a lifetime
In each moment,
Dying countless deaths,
Because it seemed
The stream of life
No longer flowed.

And so I withdrew
Under the blankets
And for a while embraced
This death in sleep.

Content With This Solitude
(2 August 2016)

Horror of horrors, what devilry this?
It's certain that something's amiss
Despite outside where air is clean
The air is putrid or so it seems
Try as I might to fill my lungs
It hurts to breathe, my body wrung
It seems as though the whole world's weight
To endure has become my fate
When I'm awake, no peace is mine
And only emptiness I find
The only solace that me greets
Is what I find 'neath crumpled sheets
But that is not a healing true
Or yet a way my heart renew
'Tis but a coward's escape slick
That promises to do the trick
But trick it does and fill with lies
The mind as it smothers my sighs
So wake I must and wakeful stay
Lest I become this trickster's prey
And praying now for fortitude
I'm content with this solitude

Into the Maelstrom
(3 August 2016)

Into the maelstrom was I dragged
And also to turmoil
One minute up, another down
My reaction – recoil

Each day passed along so smoothly
And little did I know
Soon assailed I would be greatly
And would be brought so low

Who could ever predict future
And know what time did hold
One day's warmth would yield, surrender,
The next one's dire cold

Who knew that the laughs were numbered
Or that there'd be so few
That we'd have no more occasion
Memories make anew

Taken for granted all those days
Invaluable now
Driven home that what is lost can't
Be e'er redeemed somehow

With that thought, inside the maelstrom
Tormented now I find
Regret may take up the minutes
But not give peace of mind

Inside the Maelstrom
(4 August 2016)

Inside the maelstrom, living still
If you can call this life
Surrounded now by the 'if only's
That stab just like a knife

Mulling o'er the 'could have's, 'should have's,
And yea the 'would have's too
Though knowing that stuck within time
There's nothing now to do

Present time might be quite different
If differently I chose
Contemplating all paths diverse
Self-reproach ever grows

Tossed about by thoughts that plague me
Buffeted on all sides
Sinking down dragged by the currents
No more can I abide

What prayer for me, and what hope also
How can I find release
What sacrifice needed to offer
These misgivings appease

The only hope, the only prayer,
The last speaker's not death
That mourning will surrender to joy
When draw my final breath

I Can Life Regain
(6 August 2016)

I close my eyes to face this grave darkness
And open them up so I do not see
Amidst all of life's constant distractions
The emptiness that just wants hold of me
In the darkness alone shines but dimly
A meagre light that is offering hope
But in the brightness that is all around me
Blinded by it I can only grope

I shut my ears so to greet the silence
Unstopping them would just force me to hear
All the noises that cacophonously
Drown the words that would calm all my fears
For these loud voices creating din now
Leave but a slim chance to hear a voice soft
And so only in the deafening silence
Hearing it does take my spirit aloft

So I build a wall and I close myself in
A cocoon cozy to save me I weave
Proximity with strangers around me
Highlights my isolation I believe
For all the cranky and clamoring people
Needing theater, yes, wanting so much
So that only in this deprivation
Can I yet feel what I so long to touch

So with this 'sensational' privation
With heightened senses in the face of loss
Sinking below the rough waves that assault
I take this sentence at so great a cost
Not seeing, not hearing, also not touching
No confusions that can dull the pain
Cut off from life though with those who are living
In the face of death I can life regain

A Day With Him
(6 August 2016)

Can I buy a day with him?
How much would it cost?
Can this state of penury
Get worse after this loss?
What is worthwhile, what worthless;
Priorities rearrange.
Now that there's no going back
What future still remains?

So what about a day with him?
A miracle I ask.
Is it asking for too much?
Is it too hard a task?
I think not for faith does say
The bonds of death you broke.
So one more time would be a snap
If just one word you spoke.

Won't you give a day with him?
I reckon it's futile.
Even asking for this thing
I feel the stirring bile.
For what would happen when it's time
For him to go once more?
I would ne'er withstand it then
If I've not done before

Wait For Me
(11 August 2016)

Speaking to the silence that surrounds me.
Echoes in the vacuum of my mind.
Do I speak, but speak in futility
For no one can hear these cries of mine?
In the distressed brightness of the shadows,
Blinded by the sightlessness I see
Not a single underprop. In view shows
Infinite and endless fall for me.
Grasp for you but all my fingers find full
The waning wisps of withered wishes when
I desire dreams that are delightful,
That bring you back into this world of men.
But cross this barrier you've gone and I see
Ne'er to return but sure to wait for me.

A Smile Was Placed On You
(14 August 2016)

I did not like it
The way you looked
It was not how I
Remembered your face
The cold pipe
Intruding into you
Contorting your lips,
Your mouth, your face
Nullifying your smile
And though this was you
It was not.

So I made a request
In earnestness
Asking them, imploring,
To remove the pipe
And restore to your face
The gentleness that
Endeared you to me
And they did comply
Graciously and with unction

But I looked down
On your restored face
With utter sadness
Tears streaming
In unending rivulets
Of newfound loss
For though it seemed
As though you smiled
Only I knew
It was not but that
A smile was placed on you

Once More Lend Your Ear
(15 August 2016)

Did you then know in the back of your mind
That your journey here had come to an end?
With that knowledge did you chance to find
A way with resolve for me forth to send?
Was it that you knew that try as we might
You were going on and not coming back?
Did you know that you had won the fight
And that mine had to be kept on track?
Was it for that that you sent me away
Comforting me with a future I'd like
So I'd go and say the words I'd to say
And not be concerned with holding the dike?
Those words that I said you never did hear
Wouldn't you just once more lend your ear?

Do You Remember?
(16 August 2016)

Do you remember, when I was a tot,
Needing to hold onto your hand in mine?
Whether I walked just a bit or a lot
I needed your assistance all the time.
Stumbling while walking, as I did explore,
With you I would feel no fear in my heart.
Knowing that you were behind and before
Your hands to stop if to fall I would start.
Then came the cruel day when you would go
And I held your hand in mine yet again.
Though you were sinking little did I know
That your fight was done and I hoped in vain.
But as you departed and as death did steal,
Did you in your hands my hands chance to feel?

To Dry While I Bleed
(16 August 2016)

I've trembled in despair
I'm shook to the bone
I feel in a crowd though
I'm still quite alone
I've consoled me myself
I've cajoled my thoughts
I've quieted my mind
Though I am distraught
I've wished me some wishes
I've yearned to go back
I hopelessly hope I
Can stand this attack
I've cried me an ocean
I've wept me a sea
So I string my sore heart
To dry while I bleed

I Wait Now For the Dawn
(17 August 2016)

What is it that I mourn?
What brings this sorrow near?
What pain each day reborn
Threatens to stoke the fears?

Where have you gone from me?
Is there a pleasant place
That those like you can see
Who now behold God's face?

What is it that you do?
Is there some glorious task
That defines the new
Creation? I must ask

What are these questions now?
Why do they raise their heads?
Is it I doubt to know
What waits me when I'm dead?

Nay! Confidence have I
That new life waits for us
That the end's not to die
The final state's not dust.

But what I grieve is stark
This vacuum now you're gone.
So in this deepening dark.
I wait now for the dawn.

The Day That Never Came[2]
(21 August 2016)

A new day dawns upon us now
Just as does each new day.
But not the same, and this I know,
E'en though my mind is frayed.
This day would have been the one
To see another year.
Seventy nine turns round the sun;
Our cause for joy and cheer.
But yet this joy from us denied
This mortal coil you shed.
This day has dawned, trying to bely
That you have gone ahead.
And now in its rank cruelty
It plays its vicious game.
This is the day not meant to be,
The day that never came.

---

[2] Dad would have turned 79 on Sunday, 21 August 2016. It was not to be.

Taken From Me
(26 August 2016)

Where are the pastures green?
Where are the waters still?
Where, in this vale is found,
A way to shore the will?

This vale, though full of those
Who've also lost as I,
Seems lonely for each one
Is cocooned in their sighs.

Inside this dreaded vale
A brace of months I've walked.
Cheap comforts I've refused
Though I have seen them hawked.

I continued to go
But knew not whither to.
For with no end in sight
The darkness fell anew

But as the darkness fell
This thought did come to me
That in this vale of death
With me you'll always be

And so renewed I walk
Not stumbling anymore.
Your presence has restored
The hope I'd lost before.

This hope will never fail
That with my eyes I'll see
The one you have received
But have taken from me.

When Life's Not Here
(1 September 2016)

Death, they say, is but a door
Into a world that's new.
Do you concur, was it the same
When you yourself went through?

What kind of world now waits for us
Is it a world of bliss,
Sitting on clouds and playing harps?
Please say no to this!

Or is it something darker still
And is this life just snuffed
Are we like candles in the wind
Our flames gone with a puff?

I hope not that, I hope there's more,
Or everything is lost
All our deeds, our words, our loves
Nothing! Too high a cost!

This blinking of an eye we have
To love, to hope, to praise
And love and hope and praise remain
When from the grave we're raised.

And so I know that, though you're gone,
Somehow that you're still here
And so I do not fear the day
When I that door must clear.

For I do deem that what we had
The forty seven years
That meant much then and mean much now
Must mean when life's not here.

Deludes the Soul
(2 September 2016)

Time is the healer, or so it is said,
Covering all of the wounds we have known
'Rasing the regrets of things left unsaid
Filling the vacuum that in us has grown.
Like every healing it sometimes can sting
When momentous moments just drive home the pain,
Of absence that's present. The reflection brings
A yearning remembrance, a pillow tear-stained.
But can the healing of time passing by,
From minutes to hours, and hours to years,
Completely restore each loss as it flies
Or will there always be a side that is pierced?
I reckon that time does not really make whole
Just obscures the past and deludes the soul.

Bring on the Throes
(5 September 2016)

Each sunrise brings me a day nearer you
But each new dawn brings a day that is same
Same as the one that has died with the dew
The only thing that is new is its name.
Everyday chores and the workdays alike
Present a cycle that's constant through time.
Even the weekend's rhythms, as a pike,
Drive home the lack of occasion to pine.
Days filled with everything bland, yet enhanced;
Nights on a pillow in restful unrest.
Dreaming, while wakened, insane happenstance,
Turbulent sleep, with a heart-pounding chest.
So though each sunrise is one day more close
The ones since you left still bring on the throes.

Alone Again
(10 September 2016)

Alone again with the din round me;
The P.A. system's blaring noise
For people scurrying about I see
To destinations of their choice.
Sitting, I wonder at this voyage
That we have some years to enjoy
But spend it like rats to our damage
A woeful and unfruitful ploy.
Better our values to rearrange
Learning to love what is best
For though we're restless it is strange
We all flee timeless unrest.
And in this bustle it hits home
We come here and go from alone.

Life Is A-Fleeting
(10 September 2016)

Life is a-fleeting
The days pass on by
The minutes soon turn into years
Every friends' meeting
Some far and some nigh
Lets us remember what's dear

Busy days always
But crowd out the ones
That bring meaning into one's soul
Trying to erase
Over many suns
Memories that make one whole

But given a chance
Rekindle the flame
Of friendships that never can die
We can join the dance
And quite unashamed
Bid the busy devils goodbye

To Find You Are With Me
(10 September 2016)

Thirty thousand feet up high
I'm soaring in the clouds
But does it mean I am more nigh
To you? I have my doubts.

For where you are is not a place
That is so far from us
That when we chance ourselves to raise
The distance twixt closes

For I do deem that though you've gone
You are not far but near
Near as the dawn is to the morn
I see that plain and clear

So though these miles I do ascend
I'm not an inch more close
But still my heart does not descend
Into a void morose

For I do know that where you've gone
Is where someday I'll be
And in that place I'll find my home
To find you are with me

Dying We Live
(18 September 2016)

A week gone by, since the last time I wrote
Week filled with clutter, week of the mundane,
Crowded by all that is urgent, of note,
Leaving me in its wake, driving insane
Midst the uncountable souls at the gate
Strangely alone I did find me the time
Direct my thoughts and to measure my state
Fathom anew how great this loss of mine
But now the bustle of days taken flight
Only does hustle with promises vain
For now the cycles of darkness and light
Repeat ad nauseam what is the same
So I find that life encompasses death
Each moment's dying we live drawing breath.

When Last I Will Sleep
(18 September 2016)

I still remember the times that we had
Talking and singing and laughing away;
Times of great sadness and times that were glad
Recounting stories of long gone by days.
At the parties you regaled us along;
Sonorous voice carried many a tune -
'Island in the sun', 'banana boat song' -
Carried away we would join in quite soon.
But now we have no occasion to sing
Never in years now to raise our voices
For to the island the nightfall dusk brings
And the boat song drowned in all the noises
But do you still have that voice ever deep
And will I hear it when last I will sleep?

Unhappened Wishes
(23 September 2016)

Lying awake midst the sheets in the bed,
Dying a lifetime each second it seems.
Trying to close my eyes and rest my head,
But in the silence the emptiness screams.
Just with this chance for the urgent to shrug,
Quieten my mind as the day now does end,
Then with a rushing my heartstrings to tug
Unhappened wishes that were never meant.
Sleeping while wakeful, awake while asleep;
The days dark as night, nights noisy as day.
Agonizing as the moments do creep,
A fly within amber I can only say,
"You've gone now from me, though gone to your home,
My unhappened wishes still plague me alone."

Make Amends
(24 September 2016)

Can there be joy in sorrow?
In pleasure is there pain?
Is there a new tomorrow
Or everything the same?

As each new day now passes
The same as all the old,
Time still, e'en as it marches
To futures yet untold.

We stumble and we stutter
Our way upon this rock
And our hearts still would flutter
If ever we took stock.

Yet spiralling we remain
In free fall all through life.
Can altitude be regained?
On what hope can we thrive?

Just that there's joy in sorrow
For this is not the end.
There'll be a new tomorrow
When God will make amends.

We Both Couldn't Speak
(25 September 2016)

Tomorrow will be a quarter year gone;
Three months since last heard your voice in my ear
How I have got by God knows - him alone -
Stabbing reminders that you are not here.
I still recall you last gripping my hand;
Though you in pain, you tried my pain to ease;
Sending me away issuing command
To go, return, and then your ears to please.
But 'twas not to be for I'd not the chance
To return so you'd see me by your side,
Finally happened the dread happenstance;
Life draining from you, I helpless beside.
And watching I did with tears wetting cheek,
You went from me and we both couldn't speak.

Always With You
(25 September 2016)

When you took him from me
You took him to you
So through this agony
I find comfort new

But agony still 'tis
There's no denying
Or something'd be amiss
And I'd be lying

I wait now again see
To touch and to hear
What waiting length for me
Too long I do fear

For waiting's not easy
Uphill every day
Each new day makes queasy
When hope does betray

Yet again I must wake
With hope in my heart
That you who give and take
Can see end from start

So through this agony
I find comfort new
That though he's not with me
He's always with you

Opened For You
(27 September 2016)

Three months gone by, unreality stings,
Sometimes I think I might just get a call,
That you would phone me and ask me some things -
'How are the kids?' or 'Did you see that ball?'
Stepping inside the apartment these days,
Still expect you to walk out through a door,
Humming a tune or with treats on a tray;
That we would both have the chance to talk more.
But all these wishes, how futile they are!
Raising desires to levels of hope,
Making the yearning heart ache without par,
Painting illusions, inviting to grope.
But now no doorway for you to come through,
Since the last doorway had opened for you.

Death's Worst Cannot
(29 September 2016)

Gone the explosion that shattered the heart
No more the unbelief's sudden onset
Rather a constant reminder does start
That you have gone and have slipped through life's net
Walk in a daze and I barely can see
What lies ahead and what hope can be mine
Plagued with the thought un-bedazzled I be
And this dark cloud has no silvery line
But this thought has come so full of despair
Lies all it is as it tries to kill hope
Though it assaults me I learn to beware
See through deception and onto faith grope
For through this doubt I undoubtedly see
Even death's worst cannot take you from me

Despite What's Concealed
(1 October 2016)

Only the tip's what's visible to you
What's underneath you can't see
When you look at me what comes into view
Is just a mask but not me

For what is lurking beneath the approved
What is concealed by the mask
Is what, if revealed, will lead to reproof
And I'd be taken to task

What lies beneath - all the fears and the shame,
All of the weakness that's mine -
Must not be mentioned and never be named
For it is far from sublime

So who I am is a secret to you
That I can never reveal
Unless I know I can trust you to do
'Cept me despite what's concealed

Cuts Like A Knife
(1 October 2016)

Though I again am aloft in the clouds
Still do I find that my spirit can't soar
Body in flight, yet my soul cries aloud
Making me wonder what time has in store
Missing you dearly my senses do scream
I every day see the questions arise
Battered my faith as are shattered my dreams
Welcoming nightfall but dreading sunrise
Going through motions is what I now do
Busy-ness keeps me from reflecting now
Only the diff'rent does bring into view
Desolate landscape yet living somehow
Yet 'tis not the landscape that's without life
Rather you not here still cuts like a knife

Shut To Me
(9 October 2016)

Out through the window I direct my gaze
Here on the opposite side of the Earth
Early this morning I peer through the haze
Take in the blurry view for what it's worth
What do I see, but the tops of the trees
Greener than the greenest trees I've beheld
Swaying so gently in the gentle breeze
Leaves rustling ever with stories to tell
But now these trees do my thoughts to you bend
Looking at them all the memories sink
Of how you'd find someone for to ascend
Harvest the fruit so that we all could drink
So now I gaze at these coconut trees
Wishing your presence were not shut to me

No Prayer Left For Me
(23 October 2016)

Sleeping, I dreamed of a terrible dream,
Though it had started so hopeful and true,
Laying I was on a bed quite pristine
And by my side, through worries, I saw you
There I was after the years brought down low
Brought back to life just in the nick of time
All of my past disappeared, none to show
The future unfocused, not seeming like mine.
But you were there and your hopes, your prayers
Pulled me back from the very brink of doom
And as I dreamed all the feelings came bare
Surrounded me with the darkest of gloom
For on the bed was not I, I could see
Tables were turned and no prayer left for me

From Dreams I Awake
(29 October 2016)

With not a sound you were taken from me
In silence that batters and lashes my soul.
And though I was there, still I could not be
But muted, deafened and rendered unwhole.
I scream now in silence for just one sound,
That I could perhaps once more hear your voice.
This mute cacophony spins me around;
Not hearing, my ears recoil at the noise.
What emptiness this that drives me insane,
That even now does my soul haunt in dreams
To conjure anew the desired refrain
Of words you once spoke, yet speaking it seems?
Yet each occasion does end as I quake
And into this silence from dreams I awake.

Am I Still Dreaming?
(10 November 2016)

Am I still dreaming or am I awake?
Happen to hear your voice inside my head
But it's been months now, I think and I quake
I heard your words but now silence instead
What lasting glimpse I had, what memories
Painfully watching them wheel you away
Your body inert, your eyes did not see
I saw, though helpless, to make you to stay
But you had gone ahead by then I knew
There was no joyful returning to me
Tears washed my cheeks coming fresh as the dew
Grief a prison from which I could not flee
And still in moments when left all alone
I think of that day - it burns to the bone

No One To Me
(15 November 2016)

And you have left me, yes, gone far away
In through the doorway and behind the veil.
Whirling thoughts fill me with no words to say
Thousands of questions, but answers, they fail.
Fatherless now I am, now that you've left;
Where are those arms that did hold me so strong?
Stripped of all hope I live, though I'm bereft,
Each dawn brings you nearer, but still too long.
Stumbling perpetual is now my state;
Falling forever but not hit the ground.
Mourning I remain with no tears of late;
Dried up the river and muted my sounds.
But when I see you next how will it be
In that world will you be no one to me?

Dark Is The Noon
(18 November 2016)

Early that morning I spotted the moon
Big, just as big as can be
Beautiful, circular, over me loomed
Hide and seek behind the trees

Walking my sniffing Retriever Golden
Meandering on the road
But to the circle I am beholden
Though this debt isn't a load

For the orb silver closely does follow
In the cool breeze of the dawn
In this serenity I do wallow
Wait for the day to be born

Without a care does the golden one stride
Moving from hither to yon
While above me in the clouds the moon rides
One moment seen and then gone

Looking again I do seek and I find
Source of the beams of the night
Hiding behind the dense trees in my mind
Where battle darkness and light

And as the light of the day drives the dark
Still in my mind I do see
The world though beauteous, my thoughts grow stark
Down, ever down, they drag me

For though the moon seems to sail in the clouds
I wallow low in the gloom
This thought rushes me, but don't say it loud
Without you dark is the noon.

Who Knew?
(19 November 2016)

Who knew I'd be so hollow
When you were gone from me?
Who knew each new tomorrow
Would be pure agony?
Who knew each vacant moment
Would seem so eternal?
Who knew each fresh new torment
Would wound so terminal?
Who knew I'd be so listless
Going through motions drear?
Who knew life could be blissless
Even though there's no fear?
Who knew the sunlight streaming
Could be not warm, but cold?
Who knew those bright rays beaming
Could darken, thoughts untold?
Who knew each fleeting heartbeat
Could be a long-drawn sigh?
Who knew life could be replete
With just one long-asked "why?"?

Fatherless Today I Am
(19 November 2016)

Fatherless today I am
And fatherless I'll be
Yes, fatherless forever there's no
Father here for me

And sonless you have now become
Yes, sonless from that day
And sonless you'll remain e'en though your
Son on earth does stay

Affection we had for the other
Affected us so great
Not affected is the grief that's
Affected me to date

Effective all those years have been
Their effect still remains
The effect that now moves my heart's
Effected to my gain

So though this son now has no father
And this father has no son
Still does this son rejoice for his
Father the Father won

For You There's No Grave
(23 November 2016)

No stone to be found yet to say that you lived
Or carvings declaring the day that you passed
No witty last words were on granite to give
Nor hopeful reminders eternity's vast
Everyone, dreading that they would become,
A memory lost both in time and in space
Forgotten forever amid the humdrum
Of life. Build their tombstones and set them in place
But you, ever always with different thought,
Departed, not giving these ideas wings,
Forever helpful, your body not rot
Living always in intangible things
For even in dying to others you gave
Your undying life for for you there's no grave

Each Time I Read These Poems
(28 November 2016)

Each time I read these poems
I am transported to
Relive the nascent moments
Of horrors once anew

It seems there is a millstone
Around my neck that's hung
That will remain there until
Each tear from me is wrung

The horrors rage inside me
Anguish like skin is peeled
Unrelenting ever always
Never to be repealed

Each revisited moment
That I from past let loose
Assails me as it garlands
Me with its deathly noose

And since you have departed
Time's run to a standstill
Each mem'ry's blazing fires
Frozen, but not from chill

Though I run helter-skelter
These fires to escape
The wheel of time e'er makes me
Return into their wake

So stop I now from running
To face the onslaught dread
These memories still whirling
Around inside my head

And so I read these poems
For when I read 'tis true
I am transported back to
The moments had with you

Wanting
(30 November 2016)

The sun now up, wanted, the skies have cleared
But still no warmth can penetrate this chill
That me surrounds and fills the want of fears
That what I want, I wanting ever will
For I am wanting you; want your return
Retrace the steps and come back through the door
A want futile, but will I ever learn
And will I ever want it never more?
Stubborn and unwanting the wanting truth
That there's a want of coming back for you
I set myself apart and start to brood
And drown me in a grief of want that's new
For till the grave opens and welcomes me
I'll ever want for you and wanting be

Welcome Regret's Kiss
(3 December 2016)

Some say life is short and sweet
Short and sweet is what they claim
But life is with bitters replete
Joy comes mixed with sorrow's pain
For though joy can fill with light
It gives way to sorrow's night

You were here for years too short
My eyes blinked and you were gone
Didn't know you would depart
Thought you would return to home
Then did swing the Reaper's scythe
Announcing end of your fight

I recall the minutes dear
I sat with you to plot the way
Of when, dispelled our deepest fears,
You'd be with us for all your days
But all your days were all too few
If only, only then I knew

So though I agree life is short
I dare not say that it is sweet
These few minutes of grave import
Are given for those whom we meet
And if to value them we miss
We might just welcome regret's kiss

Coming With You
(10 December 2016)

With the advancement of this year's advent
Anticipating his coming relief
Calling to mem'ry the time he was sent
Into our midst to heal all of our grief
I sit and ponder how diff'rent it is
This year's yule season from all in my past
Going through motions, though something's amiss,
A vacuum, emptiness, a void immense, vast
For this yule season is one without you
Never before have I had such a one
Most of them mirthful and merry, 'tis true,
Now no bells jingle, no now there is none
But still I wait for his coming anew
For his coming to me is a coming with you

I Wonder
(10 December 2016)

I wonder how deep it can go
This pain
Oh this pain that I feel
I wonder where from grief does grow
This fruit
Oh this fruit doesn't heal

I wonder which star-kiss-ed night
A joy
Yes a joy will yet bring
I wonder if heavenly lights
Do know
Do they know what to sing

I wonder if there is a place
For us
Yes for us when we die
I wonder its time and its space
Are found
Are they found if we try

I wonder if there is a friend
Whose arms
Yes whose arms welcome us
I wonder... The wondering ends
There's he
Yes there's he whom we trust

Emptiness Takes Flight
(11 December 2016)

Just the other day I went
To a familiar place
Where often I have gone back in the past
But it seemed so different
In, oh, so many ways
That thinking back, I think and am aghast

Brick and mortar hadn't changed
The blueprints were the same
To all appearances nothing was new
Still to me it was quite strange
As though it had been maimed
A wound that slowly, surely in it grew

There were others to be sure
Within the walls to live
A bustle filled the place with life, that's true
Still it seemed to need a cure
In shadows hid furtive
Creating a channel for the sprue

Thinking back my thoughts do hit
Upon a true belief
That sheds upon this incident some light
What I sensed that day, to wit,
The depths of all my grief
That in your absence emptiness takes flight

A Mess Before Too Long
(11 December 2016)

I thought that I could not be broke
That I would stand firm as a rock
No matter what horrors awoke
I'd not be shaken from the shock

I thought that I would never weep
And show how weak a man I am
That dried-eyed I would always sleep
I'd shed a tear e'er first I'm damned

I thought that I would nothing feel
That never once the well would flow
Of emotions my balance steal
That only temperance I'd know

I thought no matter the attack
The onslaught I would bear with ease
My defenses would never slack
To sentiment not bend my knees

But then did come the day of griefs
That tested me and proved me wrong
Defenses fell like falling leaves
I was a mess before too long

One Day At Last
(31 December 2016)

So as this year grinds to an end
And served its share of grief
A loss too great to comprehend
That permits no relief

I think of the six months gone by
Since I was ripped to shreds
My heart attacked, strung out to dry
My hopes, unraveled threads

Every day I think of you
Wishing that you were here
But only wishes can't renew
The hope now disappeared

The only thought that comforts me
Is that you suffered less
Your time of pain was not lengthy
And you've gone to your rest

So though with grief I struggle still
This year crawls to the past
And I remain, knowing I will
See you one day at last

My Saint Nick
(31 December 2016)

As a child Christmas would raise up the hope
I'd not be missed out by good ol' Saint Nick
That he would find in his bag when he groped
The gift that, for me, he had long planned to pick
And over the years I grew up and I shed
The childish illusions surrounding the gifts
I shrugged off the thoughts of a man dressed in red
And knew who for me ever did forswear thrift
Every year my Nick would lavish on me
Things I desired and what brought me joy
But more than that my Nick would cause me to see
The source of the gifts was his love for his boy
But now this Christmas has gone into past
The first one without my Nick and not the last

Suddenly Taken Away
(31 December 2016)

Suddenly you have been taken from me
Suddenly you were not here
And though six months have gone by I can see
It's always too sudden I fear

For I know now that no matter the length
A time I was gi'en to prepare
Would have been too short, and would have sapped my strength
Leaving me sore from my care

It was just a blink of an eye that took you
I wish I could unblink it now
But that's just a wish that's futile and untrue
To recede to the past somehow

But life goes on and so also does time
Relentlessly marking it's beat
Giving no reason, nor giving its rhyme
Giving no place to retreat

And trapped within time and in space as am I
I shoulder this burden each day
That I continue on this earth till I die
Be suddenly taken away

New Life For Dead Dreams
(5 January 2017)

New year begins with its promise
Like all the years in the past
That 'twill be one I would cherish
And to this hope I hold fast

But the year gone by had also
To me its promises swear
That I a turnaround would know
Fortunes would come, not despair

But its promises were empty
Broken complete in its midst
Leaving a challenge aplenty
Shards of the hopes I had wished

Still they lie strewn here around me
Daring me to pick them all
And so I go down on bent knee
Collecting both great and small

So, as a beggar, I amass
What once was whole, now in bits
Won'dring if this pain will e'er pass
Questioning in starts and fits

Can hope that's shattered be renewed?
In grief can there shine a beam?
Can each day with joy be imbued?
Is there new life for dead dreams?

The Darkness Can't Prevail
(10 January 2017)

As, today, the dawn attempts to break;
The sun, in vain, its light pierce through the clouds
The cool of night still lingers, in its wake
I think of you, but silently, not loud.
For as the heat of sun battles the cold
And the light of day wars with the night
A weight, a shroud, on me settles untold
Giving wings to wishes taken flight
But as these wishes 'way from me do fly
New hope descends on me with its embrace
For through the clouds so dense does catch my eye
A beam, though narrow, yet that's filled with grace
For it says though thick is the night's veil
Still faced with light the darkness can't prevail

End Of Time
(10 January 2017)

Still the darkness lasts, renewed the fight
And clouds once more do cover up the sun
The beam of hope has gone, as has its light
Failing in its task, this single one
Is it true that there be ups and downs
Forever as do battle dark and light
Or is there vict'ry as the morning crowns
Each day's dawning, dispelling the night?
And who knows what answers do us await?
Who even knows what questions we must ask?
And who knows where we go in the next state
Or even if for us there is a task?
But even through this questioning hope shines
In looking forward to the end of time

Counting The Days
(12 January 2017)

Time moves on slowly with dragging of feet
Every lived moment moves into the past
Though we can't stop it we can make the sweet
Mem'ries that make what is fleeting to last
And so I think of those days had with you
Before you were taken from me afar
Before what settled was darkness not dew
Before the making of mem'ries was marred
Listened your voice filled with sweetness to me
Would that I could hear with words said anew
But all I have is the mem'ries I see
And the reliving of moments too few
So till the skies split with heavenly rays
This life I live is just counting the days

Listless
(26 January 2017)

Listless I am though is vibrant the day
Darkened this cloud that has fallen on me
The moments pass slowly and wither away
I peer through the darkness but just cannot see
Seven months gone in the blinking of eyes
Though every moment stretched eternally
And in my dreams live my hopes and my sighs
A yearning to go back to what cannot be
And every night as my eyes I do close
The visions of yesterdays dance in my mind
Visions of longing as hea'en only knows
But daylight discloses through visions I'm blind
And so the long days circle endlessly
As listless I am, e'en so listless I'll be

Provoked
(12 February 2017)

Provoked were all my tears summoned today
Raw now these wounds that had started to heal
Unwelcome, unanticipated, and frayed
All the emotions rushed for me to feel
Gazing at one more now taken in death
Witnessed my mind reaching back into time
When I, with you as you drew your last breath,
Hopelessly hoped for a wonder sublime
But was no wonder for me on that day
You slipped away and did summon my tears
There was no levee to hold them at bay
As in a moment you went far from near
Once again today these feelings came raw
Opened and provoked by all that I saw

I Let Myself Weep
(13 February 2017)

When you were taken from me people came
Showing their sorrow and also their tears
Crowding me, stifling me, driving insane
Wondering why 'twas my eyes remained clear
For when you went all the tears did arise
No one around I did permit them flow
But later under the questioning eyes
I found my sorrow I just could not show
But then the day came when others in pain
Drew 'way from me every questioning gaze
That now began driving others insane
Giving me what I wanted - sorrow's space
And so as others faced grave sorrows deep
In plain sight I hid and I let myself weep

Fall On Deaf Ears
(14 February 2017)

Three years ago you were quite tense
Not knowing the outcome
If I'd emerge with any sense
Or if I would be numb

The hours went by but lost to me
For you the ages stretched
Not knowing what insanity
Would render me quite wretched

What pain was yours I know quite well
For there would come a time
When tables turned my pain to spell
And time to pray was mine

What worries did furrow your brow
Those worries furrowed mine
Not knowing if healing somehow
Would be given this time

Those worries were in prayer expressed
To remove all the fears
Yours were heard in your distress
Did mine fall on deaf ears?

Just Become Blue
(22 February 2017)

I see the sky and its sparkling azure
Think of the aquamarine of the sea
Cobalt, the metal, but when it is pure
Precious topaz that is pale as can be
Then there are blooms like the cornflower bright
Indigo also comes up in my mind
Periwinkle lends a soft fragile sight
Just like the lavender that you may find
So many shades are there, what do they say
Palest to brightest and lightest to dark
Ever-y moment in night or in day
Unveiled emotions are captured when stark
But in this world that is now without you
All of these shades merge and just become blue

A Moment Of All Goodbyes
(9 March 2017)

Ask me, I beg of you, ask me today
Seek my response to your questioning mind
Request to know when I'm mute, what to say
And what to see when hopeless I am blind
Sit with me here with my barren thoughts now
Fruitlessly waiting for spring of new life
Hopelessly hoping that someday, somehow
Living will not be the stab of a knife
But midst the stabbing time carries me on
Refusing moments to rest and renew
Crowding me daily at dusk and at dawn
Lest I realize one plain thing so true
That when you went 'twas as though, to my eyes,
'Twas to me a moment of all goodbyes

Three Quarters
(26 March 2017)

Three quarters of a year has gone
Slipped silent to the past
This nine month long gestation
Proved fruitless and too fast
For how could these thirty nine weeks
Bring solace to my heart
When now the wishes unfulfilled
Remain before they start

What frailty this, how transient we
Are given too few years
To learn to love, to accept grace,
To overcome our fears
Upon this spinning topsy top
We welcome each new dawn
Not knowing when or how or where
We'll see our final morn

Deceived are we to think there are
A plenty brand new days
To wake up to, to draw our breath
And yes to mend our ways
But looking back I **see** without
A warning you were gone
A blinking eye was all it took
And here I am forlorn

One Unheard Voice
[to be sung to the tune of O Love That Wilt Not Let Me Go]
(30 April 2017)

Four dozen times has come this day
And gone into the past
How many more will come my way
I cannot tell my nerves do fray
For thinking of the last

This one did come with wishes true
From friends and kith and kin
It started when the day was new
Was fresh just like the morning dew
Before the beams shone in

From all around the globe they came
Rang sweetly in my ear
The countless people saying my name
I basked in this my day of fame
That told me I was dear

A chorus loud did sing for me
With its refrain repeat
I thankful that I chanced to be
Alive for this new day to see
With gratitude replete

Just one thing now does mar this tune
And raise a dinning noise
That though these wishes were a boon
Amidst the melodious fune
Was just one unheard voice

If Only
(1 May 2017)

If only I had known
That you would no more wish
If only I were shown
The future barren, bleak
If only I could sense
That something was amiss
If only I knew whence
What rendered you so weak

If only I heard then
The words that you did say
If only I knew when
Your heart would suffer harm
If only I were told
The number of your days
If only I could hold
You warm within my arms

If only I could dare
To storm the doors of hea'n
If only I would bare
My broken heart once more
If only I would ask
A year or maybe ten
If only I could bask
In blissfulness of yore

If only all these things
For me would come to pass
If only then I'd sing
With joyfulness again
I soon would end the song
For we're as blades of grass
You'd go before too long
I wrecked once more with pain

Real And No Dream
(17 June 2017)

One circle around the gold sun we have gone
Twelve silver moons since we last saw your face
The weeks, with their rhythms, have dragged on and on
The days passed on by with an uneven pace
For some moments rushed on, while some lingered still
Determined by how brimming was the moment
Languid were some, others poignant and filled,
But filled were they all with one constant torment
For what every moment did hammer away
The bare, stark reminder of what we had lost
That cold, dark eventime on a cold and dark day
When you were taken from us at a great cost
So still we live through each moment it seems
Just hoping that it was all real and no dream

Shroud Me Again
(25 June 2017)

I sit in silence and think of the year
That has rushed me by and created these wounds
That deign to stay unhealed, still crystal clear,
Despite the waxing and waning of moons
Fresh are they still with no sign of being healed
Unseen yet far are they from being unfelt
Hurting as though my skin were being peeled
Leaving behind everyday a new welt
And so wond'ring when in silence I sit
I'll see your face again beaming with light
For then the pain will be gone, each last bit,
Dissolved at last at the long-yearned-for sight
But until then I will welcome this pain
And let your mem'ries to shroud me again

Tears Us Apart
(26 June 2017)

What is this thing that we call a laugh?
This one strangely human thing that we do
If once we hear it we can't get enough
And once we start, we quiver like dew

What is this thing that we call a smile?
The curving of lips that we long to see
Quietly it spans a distance of miles
Within its embrace we sore long to be

But there are times when the laughs and smiles rise
Forced and quite shallow and not from the heart
Coerced to conquer the deepest of sighs
But vanquished by the grief that tears us apart

You Look With Love At Me
(4 February 2018)

And in your empty eyes
I saw embrace of death
How deeply could I sigh
As you drew your last breath
Those eyes once warm to me
Stared at me dead and cold
I left behind, you free,
Now earned your crown of gold
I shudder when I think
Of how you slipped away
Your lifesigns, they did sink,
On that, your final day
But yet to me it seems
You live eternally
For still within my dreams
You look with love at me

And Yet Beside You
(7 March 2018)

I knew that you were going
Could tell the time had come
For you to taste the knowing
Of him in your new home
And yet beside you I did pray
In desperation that you'd stay

Your lifesigns, they were sinking,
Your breath so soft you breathed
Despite the machine's linking
You approached your reprieve
And yet beside you I did sing
To taste once more the joy you bring

Your eyes that ever loved me
Now with death looked so filled
For you're not there I could see
Your heart was fin'ly stilled
And yet beside you I did grope
Within that hopelessness for hope

Your skin now to my touch cold
I now knew how death felt
Relentless and ever bold
Though final blow was dealt
And yet beside you I did praise
The one who graced me with your grace

The goodbyes I could ne'er say
Were still said nonetheless
You went ahead on your way
I left with my distress
And yet beside you I did release
You to his arms and found my peace

Made in the USA
Columbia, SC
15 January 2024